W9-BYT-753

MISSION: EARTH

MISSION: EARTH

VOYAGE TO THE HOME PLANET

JUNE A. ENGLISH   THOMAS D. JONES

SCHOLASTIC PRESS
NEW YORK

For Liz, who made the voyage possible,
and Annie and Bryce, who made it important.

For Elizabeth, a believer in dreams,
even the improbable ones.

Acknowledgments

Many extraordinary people were involved in the making of *Mission:Earth*, and the authors would like to personally acknowledge their efforts.

Two superb teams joined forces to make the missions described on these pages a success. Our thanks go first to the international team of scientists and engineers who designed and built the Space Radar Laboratory, then conducted two spectacular expeditions to explore our planet. The ground team's hopes and energy were represented in orbit by the two astronaut crews who flew *Endeavour* on these voyages of discovery. We owe much to these space-based members of the expedition — without their excellence in operating *Endeavour* and the Space Radar Lab, and their keen eye as Earth observers, the radar and photographic images seen here could never have been shared with Earth's inhabitants. As crewmates, no better companions could be found for these missions to planet Earth.

To collect the results of the work done on the SRL missions into a book, we relied on yet another gifted team. David Turner used his considerable graphic skills to give the images from the mission a clear and exciting format. Jennifer Riggs and Nicole Valaire answered myriad questions and kept track of the unending details involved in putting the book together. Julie Winterbottom read the manuscript in its infant stages and gave us courage to keep working on it. Finally, Kate Waters, our vigilant editor, structured and fine-tuned *Mission: Earth* into a finished volume. We owe her special thanks for her advocacy of this book, and for the patience and understanding she used in bringing it to life.

J. E. and T. J.

Library of Congress Cataloging-in-Publication Data

English, June A.
Mission: Earth: voyage to the home planet / June A. English, Thomas D. Jones.
p.   cm.
ISBN 0-590-48571-7
1. Earth sciences — Remote sensing. 2. Astronautics in earth sciences. I. Jones, Thomas D. II. Title.
QE33.2.R4E54   1996   550′.28 — dc20   95-17474
CIP

12 11 10 9 8 7 6 5 4 3 2 1   6 7 8 9/9 0 1/0

Printed in Singapore   46

First printing, September 1996

Part of the job of every United States astronaut is to educate people about our country's space program.
Thomas Jones will not receive financial compensation from sales of this book.

Contents

Introduction

I first dreamed of leaving this planet in 1965, when U.S. astronauts began practicing for the first trips to the Moon. In our elementary school classroom, my coauthor, June English, and I watched each *Gemini* launch and splashdown along with our classmates. I am not so sure anyone else in our class was really taken with the idea of being blasted into space atop a converted military missile. But I was hooked.

By the time our astronauts reached the Moon's surface in 1969, I was sure I wanted to study science, learn to fly, and travel into space myself. As a high school student, I remember being distinctly worried that the first astronauts would reach Mars before I even had a chance to send in my application.

My fears didn't materialize. The frenzy to reach other planets slowed. Our attentions shifted closer to home, from the Moon and Mars to the Blue Planet, Earth. We now knew that our natural resources, which had once seemed inexhaustible, were limited and irreplaceable. Even as we found our environment was at risk, we were also realizing what an incredibly unique planet Earth was. We had finally begun to value our home; now we needed to learn to protect it.

While still planning trips to new worlds, NASA and other space agencies began to use space to explore our own Earth. The space shuttle was designed to be a part of this exploration: It tested its abilities in orbit even as I tested my wings as an Air Force pilot. I completed my science education just as the shuttle turned from launching satellites to its present role as an orbiting science platform. I realized my dream of being an astronaut in 1990, just in time to train as a Mission Specialist — a scientist-astronaut — for a Mission to Planet Earth.

While I'd been preparing for aviation, science, and spaceflight, June English had been sharpening her pencils and her skills as a writer. From her desk in New York City, she called me one day in the early 1990s to track down some facts for her latest science article. Our conversation turned to my upcoming shuttle mission, the first flight of the Space Radar Laboratory. My crew's studies of Earth from the shuttle *Endeavour* seemed a natural topic for June to write about, but she surprised me when she asked me to work with her in telling that story.

After seeing Earth's incredible beauty from orbit, and exploring it continent by continent for over three weeks on two 1994 Space Radar Lab missions, I realized I had plenty to say and could hardly wait to put this book together.

The images that follow, taken by *Endeavour's* advanced radar as well as the crew's film cameras, tell a story about our planet that hasn't been told in quite the same way before. My story of the mission — and June's explanation of some of the ecology of our planet — will, we hope, bring to life one of the most exciting space adventures ever.

The space program has given me an incredible gift: 22 days in orbit, soaring 135 miles above the earth. But the space program has given all of us an even greater gift: the chance to look at our planet while we're living on it. It's a great home, our home — our first and our last.

Tom Jones
Houston, Texas

A Picture of Earth

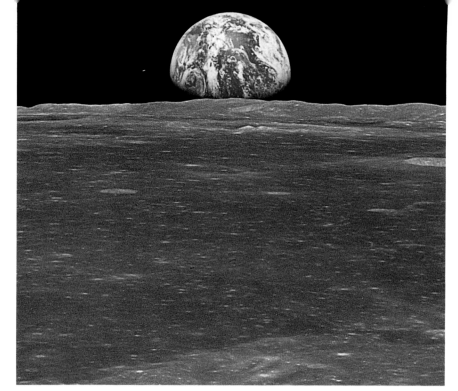

This view of the whole Earth came from the *Apollo* missions to the moon. For the first time, we could see the richness of our planet set against the starkness of space.

Modern humans have lived on Earth for around 40,000 years, but until this century, no human had ever seen the earth as a whole. Of course, people could see pieces of it: the turquoise waves of the Pacific, the swept dunes of the Sahara, the jagged spine of the Alps. But no one had ever seen Earth as a *planet*. Was it, as some ancients suggested, being held up by huge turtles? Or balancing on giant pillars? Were we really just floating out there without *anything* attached? What color was this planet and was it really round like a ball or shaped more like an avocado or pear?

Just over 25 years ago, we finally got the chance to see our planet from space. NASA's *Apollo* program, whose mission was to send a man to the Moon, gave us another surprise, a picture of our home. Circling the Moon, over 240,000 miles away, the *Apollo* astronauts photographed the whole spinning planet. Earth was a near-perfect sphere, brilliant blue-white and more dramatic than anyone had imagined.

Around the same time that we finally saw the earth, we began to realize that the planet we lived on was going through some changes. Humans, who hadn't made too much of an impact on the planet for the last 40,000 years or so, had made some serious dents in the past 100. We had changed the earth's landscape, leveling miles of forests, strip-mining ores and minerals, and tapping fuels from under the ground.

While cars and factories had improved our lives in many ways, fuel wastes were making the air dangerous to breathe and hurting delicate fish in freshwater. Though we lived on an incredibly rich and beautiful planet, we had dumped garbage nearly everywhere, *uglifying* the landscape and polluting rivers and oceans. Scientists had even created nuclear fuels and weapons that were risky to have around, which wouldn't decompose for tens of thousands of years.

If humans were having a hard time with all the changes on Earth, animals were faring even worse. About a quarter of the species on Earth were in danger of disappearing altogether. More and bigger fishing boats were depleting the supplies of ocean fish. As more people needed room to live, other land animals and plants were finding fewer and fewer places to thrive.

It was obvious some damage was being done to the planet, but we weren't sure how much or whether that damage could be undone. Even people who agreed *something* should be done argued about which were the most serious problems and where to start.

NASA and other international space agencies had been studying the earth and its environment since the late 1950s. But after the *Apollo* program, studies of the atmosphere, oceans, land, ice, and snow accelerated. In the 1980s, scientists began to take measurements from shuttle flights as well as from robot satellites. They began looking at vegetation all over the earth — where trees and crops were growing, and where they were disappearing.

During this last decade people began to realize that our atmosphere was changing. Scientists began to suspect that less vegetation and more air pollutants might be causing the earth's temperature to rise. The idea of an intensified greenhouse effect — where trapped gases in the atmosphere heat up the planet — began to develop.

Scientists also began to notice that the layer of ozone that covered the planet and protected it from solar radiation was also becoming thinner. Over parts of Antarctica a hole in the ozone layer was forming.

Seen from space, Earth was still as magnificent as it looked from the mountains of the Moon. But scientists had begun to see some of the problems of the home world. NASA, along with several international space agencies and, eventually, Russia, began forming a program to take a complete look at what was happening to the earth's environment.

Today, that program is known as the Mission to Planet Earth. This mission will use instruments in space and on the ground to identify Earth's changes. With careful measurements, scientists hope to figure out which of Earth's changes are natural and which are caused by human behavior. Mission to Planet Earth began in 1991 and will continue into the twenty-first century.

The Space Radar Lab (SRL) flights are an important part of this mission. On the following pages you can read a description of two SRL flights in the words of Tom Jones, an astronaut who flew on the missions. In the second half of the book you can take a look at what space agencies around the world have learned about the changes in our planet so far. And you can find out what scientists hope to discover as the Mission to Planet Earth continues.

This image of Earth was put together using satellites as well as ground instruments. The different colored areas show different levels of vegetation on the planet. Light brown means little or no vegetation. Yellow to orange indicates slight to medium vegetation. Heavy vegetation is represented in green.

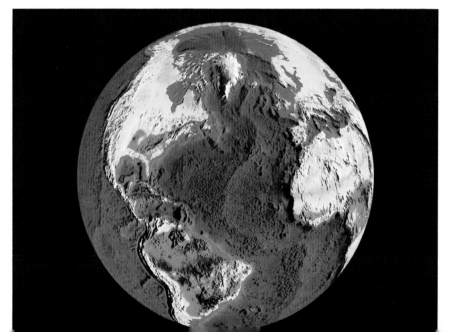

The *Endeavour* Mission: Space Radar Lab 1

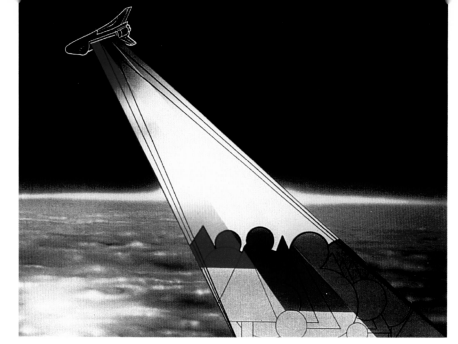

The special radar used on the Space Radar Lab (SRL) flights records Earth in three different bands or wavelengths.

When the space shuttle program started, astronauts had the equipment and the opportunity to take thousands of spectacular pictures of the earth. These photographs provided one good way of tracking changes on the surface of the planet. Pictures taken from shuttle flights and satellites during the 1980s were dramatic, revealing a perspective of the earth unlike any seen before. But the images, though they were spectacular, were incomplete. Over certain areas of the earth, the presence of clouds, snow, and other weather and light conditions obscured the landscape.

Scientists began to use radar and other sensing instruments to get at the information that simple photography missed. Though cameras and film could see the tops of things, there was a lot of information underneath the clouds and vegetation that remained invisible.

The Space Radar Lab (SRL), a combined effort by U.S., Italian, and German scientists, was designed to fix this problem. Unlike earlier space radars, SRL would include three "colors" or bands of radar energy. The X-band would measure upper vegetation zones such as forest canopies. The C-band would collect information on the central or middle vegetation zone: the trunks of trees, for instance. The L-band would gather data on the lower vegetation zones such as forest floors.

The combination of the three different radar echoes would help scientists get a complete picture of Earth. With it, they would be able to see through clouds; underneath dry, packed sand; and beneath dense forests. For the first time, a complete picture of Earth's complicated surface could be made.

NASA decided on two shuttle missions to give the Space Radar Lab a look at two different Earth seasons. *Space Transportation System (STS)-59* would be first. *Endeavour* would lift off in April of 1994 with six astronauts aboard. Sidney (Sid) Gutierrez would command *Endeavour*. Kevin Chilton would act as pilot. Linda Godwin would be Payload Commander, in charge of science onboard. Mission Specialists Rich Clifford, Jerome (Jay) Apt, and Thomas (Tom) Jones would be responsible with Linda for running the radar and pollution experiments.

In addition to the radar, another instrument, MAPS (Measurement of Air Pollution from Satellites), would be carried aboard *Endeavour*. MAPS would measure carbon monoxide pollution as it traveled through the atmosphere. This gas is carried from industry and fires on the ground into the upper atmosphere on thunderstorm updrafts.

Though *Endeavour* would pass over much of the surface of the earth, the radar measurements would be concentrated on 19 "supersites" across the planet. The supersites were spots chosen by the science team for intense study, representing Earth's changing ecology, geology, and oceans. Space Radar Lab would chart forests in Michigan, North Carolina, and the Amazon basin. It would measure snow and floodwaters in Austria, Oklahoma, Brazil, and Italy. It would look at rainfall in the Western Pacific, penetrate the sands of the Sahara, and map the lava rocks of the Galápagos. It would chart the Southern Ocean and the currents of the North Atlantic. In Australia and northern Europe, the radar would be used to make the first topographical maps from space. The radar would "see" the planet more clearly than it had ever been seen before.

The Space Radar Lab, a product of American, German, and Italian scientists, shown in action in space. A special air-pollution sensor, MAPS, sits in front of the flat radar antennae.

THE LAUNCH OF *ENDEAVOUR*

Two years of training are over, but the last three hours of the countdown seem identical to our many rehearsals over the past year. Strapped inside *Endeavour*'s crew cabin, it's difficult to believe that in a few minutes I'm going to be hurled into space aboard a 120-ton machine accelerating to a speed eight times faster than a rifle bullet.

Whatever questions we have about the reality of this morning's events are answered once and for all near the end of the countdown, when *Endeavour* comes alive. We feel the vibration of the hydraulic power units starting just five minutes before launch. Then *Endeavour* lurches abruptly as the ship's computers flex wing flaps and rudder, and swivel the main engines through one last test cycle. The shuttle is poised to go. At T-minus six seconds, *Endeavour*'s computers command the start of her three main engines. We sense the surge of rocket thrust shaking the vehicle and hear the scream of those engines ten stories beneath us. Six seconds tumble by while the crew waits for the computers to check engine performance, and then —

The launch tower outside my hatch window turns yellow-white. The reflected glare is from the twin solid rocket boosters igniting at T-minus zero. I'm shoved up, left, right, forward, and back all at once as we surge off the launch pad, powered upward by seven and a half million pounds of rocket thrust.

Already going 100 miles per hour, *Endeavour* powers past the launch tower. I watch the dark Florida landscape whirl

A synopsis of mission facts for *STS-59*:

LAUNCH DATE/SITE:	**April 9, 1994/Kennedy Space Center PAD 39A**
LAUNCH TIME:	**7:05 A.M. EDT**
ORBITER:	***Endeavour***
ORBIT/INCLINATION:	**120 nautical miles/57 degrees**
MISSION DURATION:	**11 days, 5 hours, 9 minutes, 30 seconds**
LANDING TIME/DATE:	**12:54 P.M. EDT April 20, 1994**
LANDING SITE:	**Edwards Air Force Base, California**
***STS-59* CREW:**	**Sidney M. Gutierrez, Commander**
	Kevin P. Chilton, Pilot
	Linda Godwin, Payload Commander
	Jerome Apt, Mission Specialist 1
	Rich Clifford, Mission Specialist 2
	Thomas D. Jones, Mission Specialist 4
	Red Shift: Gutierrez, Chilton, Godwin
	Blue Shift: Apt, Clifford, Jones
Cargo Bay Payloads:	**Space Radar Laboratory 1 (SRL-1)**

Endeavour vaults from Kennedy Space Center in Florida at dawn on April 9, 1994. Its mission: a new exploration of planet Earth.

crazily out the side hatch as we roll over, along the track toward orbit. The whipsaw motions of liftoff settle into a steady shaking. About 30 seconds after launch we throttle back the main engines. This reduces the stresses on *Endeavour* as we punch through the sound barrier in the thick lower atmosphere. Safely through, the computers command full thrust again. In the cabin it feels as if they've stomped on the accelerator — I'm shoved back in my seat as the shuttle surges forward. The message from *Endeavour*: "Let me show you what it *really* means to ride a rocket."

The G-forces slowly build up as 2.2 million pounds of rocket fuel are converted into forward thrust. Close to two minutes past launch and we're squeezed back into our seats at 2.5 Gs, two and a half times the force of gravity. We are moving close to 4,000 miles per hour. Then the thrust lessens as the solid rockets exhaust their fuel. I watch the clock, waiting for separation. The noise comes — a solid, metallic *klong!* as explosive bolts shear the rockets from the external tank. They fall away toward the ocean. From our seats in the mid-deck, Payload Commander Linda Godwin and I can only feel and hear the separation. Upstairs, though, our crewmates can look forward through the cabin windows. They see *Endeavour* fly right through the fireball from the small rockets that peel the empty boosters away from the orbiter.

The main engines alone now push us forward, drinking fuel from the external tank at an incredible rate, so fast they would empty a backyard swimming pool in 25 seconds. Ever lighter, we accelerate and the ride now seems impossibly smooth.

Seven minutes into our ride we reach an acceleration three times the force of gravity. I'm flattened into my chair back,

---

Sid Gutierrez, our soft-spoken, steady commander, kept our crew relaxed through a year of training with his easy sense of humor. Here he floats beneath our overhead windows with two of our Earth observation cameras. The ocean streams by 134 miles below.

Kevin Chilton and Linda Godwin collect Earth images on film. Linda, our cheerful and thorough payload commander, created a successful plan for dividing the crew's duties in orbit. Kevin, *Endeavour*'s expert pilot in space, is also a fast friend on Earth.

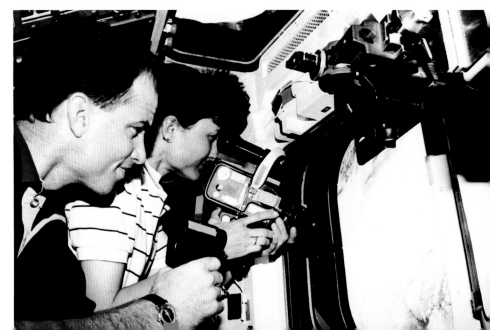

Eating in space poses some real challenges. The trick is to find something tasty that will stay glued together. This tortilla with chicken and salsa fills the bill.

DAY ONE

Time in space is precious. We have Space Radar Lab up and running in just a few hours. All of our cameras are full of film, waiting only for us to begin. While our crew is ready for work, we can't ignore the fact that we are in space. At first I feel clumsy in microgravity, bumping into walls, losing track of pens and notebooks, and wondering if I will ever have an appetite again. But in a few hours I feel at home. After a quick breakfast of Mexican scrambled eggs and some sausage, I head for the flight deck. Rich Clifford and Jay Apt and I wade in among the maps and cameras and data recorders. The Space Radar Lab is humming. Earth is waiting, and there's little time to dawdle. For the next ten days our lives will be organized minute to minute. Twelve hours are devoted to work, four hours to housekeeping (that includes eating, bathing, and shuttle maintenance). The remaining eight hours we're supposed to sleep.

All of us had spent dozens of hours in the flight simulator back in Houston. *Endeavour* at work seems nearly identical to the simulator. But there is no mistaking this new view of Earth. We juggle our eight flight-deck cameras, jockeying for the best view of the planet through windows that suddenly seem tiny. Between passes over our radar targets (the deserts of western China, sand dunes of Mongolia, ocean currents off Japan), we update *Endeavour*'s computers to pivot the shuttle into the best observing angle. We'll be circling the planet once every 89 minutes, about 16 times each day.

my suit and I weighing almost 700 pounds. Breathing is difficult — I have to force the air into my lungs against the weight of suit and parachute harness. *Endeavour*'s computers throttle back the engines to keep us under 3 Gs, which is all the shuttle's lightweight structure is built to take. We hurtle forward at 3 Gs for a very long 90 seconds, until we approach orbital velocity. We are now moving at 25 times the speed of sound, about 17,000 miles per hour. My crew watches the computer screen for the cutoff signal. Precisely on time, the main engines thunder into silence. We coast, going from 3 Gs to free fall in under a second. The pressure disappears from my chest. I'm light in my straps and so happy I yell to Linda across the mid-deck: "We're here! We're alive!"

Another metallic *bang!* as the external fuel tank separates from under our feet, drifting away from *Endeavour*. I pull off a glove and watch it tumble lazily in front of me, the final proof that I'm really *in space*.

Upside Down and Backward

We can barely tear our eyes away from the scene outside. The sun is so bright in the black of space that we can only watch it for a few seconds at sunrise and sunset before we have to turn away from the glare. But we can't help it — that's when the sun and atmosphere take on all the colors of the rainbow. Luckily a sunrise or sunset comes every 45 minutes as we pass from Earth's light hemisphere to its dark side and then back into daylight. Easier on the eyes is the clean, thin crescent of the Moon, emerging from the delicate blue of the atmosphere a few minutes before the sun wipes the night away.

Endeavour is actually upside down in orbit: its radar and pollution sensor are pointed up out of the payload bay, looking "down" at Earth. Inside the cabin, we look "up" out of our windows at Earth, rolling by overhead. The geography is a little tricky to figure out — we are streaking around the planet upside down and backward. To ease the view, we float upside down in the windows, our bodies parallel to *Endeavour*'s floor. Soon the oceans and continents begin to resemble that familiar classroom globe.

During the first full day at work in space, we see Siberia still locked in winter, the largest expanse of ice and snow on Earth. As we snap away with our cameras, our radar maps the largest forests on the planet, the northern belt of fir trees running from Moscow east to the Pacific. One of our missions is to measure how much carbon is locked up in those millions of acres of northern pines and firs. This measurement will tell us how much carbon dioxide will be added to the atmosphere

Snow clings to fence lines across frozen Siberian farmland. The melting snow and emerging fields give this Russian landscape a 3-D appearance.

if any of these forests are burned or cut down. Off Asia's east coast, we track the spring breakup of ice in the Sea of Okhotsk, west of Kamchatka, a measurement which will help scientists study global warming trends.

Southern Lights

I deliberately stay up past bedtime to watch our spectacular pass over the deserts of the Middle East. Skimming low over Iraq, we photograph fires burning in the marshes near the mouth of the Euphrates River, signs of conflict in a country still torn by civil war. At the head of the Persian Gulf, we can still see the sooty, three-year-old scars of oil-well fires set during the Gulf war, now just dark blotches lightly dusted with sand from the surrounding desert. As we soar southeast toward Antarctica and sleep, I am hypnotized by the Southern Lights, or Aurora Australis, shimmering fingers of green light reaching up from the dark ocean, an arc of light around the South Magnetic Pole.

Marshes burn near the Kuwait/Iraq border. Drainage channels in Iraq divert water from these marshes, which were set afire in internal fighting following the 1991 Persian Gulf war.

As we sweep through the night just below Australia and New Zealand, the Aurora Australis, or Southern Lights, appears. Auroras occur when charged particles from the Sun strike atoms in the atmosphere and cause them to glow.

DAYS TWO AND THREE

I wake from eight hours of sleep feeling refreshed, though my lower back is a little sore. When Rich Clifford measures me this morning, I've grown four centimeters in 48 hours! That stretching of my spine resulted from the weightlessness I'd experienced here in orbit. My muscles were stretched, too, and I have to take some medicine to ease the soreness.

I'd woken up really hungry today so the first item on the agenda is breakfast. Today's menu offered blueberries in granola and milk, two pouches of orange juice — drunk through a straw — and a handful of dried peaches. Satisfied, I'm ready to get to work.

The Ring of Fire

Today the daylight portions of our orbits carry us over Asia again. We focus our radar and cameras on dozens of sites in Russia, China, India, and Japan. We want to look at the amount of snow covering the Himalayas. The depth of the snow will give us an idea of how much water will melt into the rivers of Tibet and India come spring.

We also want to study the climate of the Mongolian and Chinese deserts and active volcanoes on the Kamchatka peninsula along the Pacific. (One of these volcanoes would *actually erupt* during our next Space Radar Lab mission, though we hadn't a clue about the upcoming drama as we photographed the area from above.) Mt. Klyuchevskaya on the Kamchatka Peninsula has dusted its summit with a dark blanket of ash, easily visible from space. The mountain is more or less inaccessible to scientists on Earth, so our photos and radar images would be the best source of information on this potentially violent spot.

Over southern Japan, we spot a plume of steam trailing from Mt. Sakurijima, and our radar charts lava deposits at other volcanoes along this Pacific Ring of Fire. This is an area of high volcanic activity that stretches in an arc along the western and eastern Pacific — from Indonesia to the western coast of the Americas.

Our radar graphically shows the area around the Mt. Klyuchevskaya volcano on the Kamchatka Peninsula in Russia. This image was made on our second flight. The dark blue triangular peak in the center of the image began erupting on September 30, 1994. The bright red areas indicate unvegetated, snow-covered ground. Green streaks mark the new ash and mudflows from the eruption.

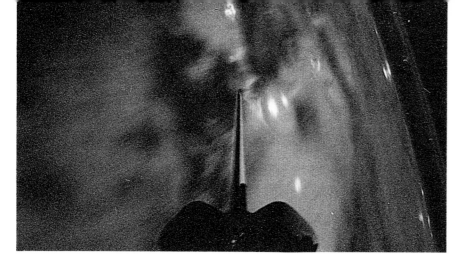

Watching storms from above is one of the highlights of all shuttle missions. Here lightning flashes through thunderstorms below the shuttle on an earlier mission.

Storms in Space

During our orbital nights we cross again and again over South America and Africa. We stay busy searching for fires and lightning. We report the positions of glowing fires and major storms to the MAPS scientists on the ground, who plot them on their charts.

Maybe more than any other sight from space, lightning gives the decided impression that the earth is alive, a living organism. The flashes from individual storm cells pop like flashbulbs from the darkness below. Bolts from within dense clouds light up entire storms for a microsecond. Even more dramatic is the behavior of lightning in long lines of storms: lightning strokes in one cloud seem to trigger a flash in a neighboring storm. The pulses then ripple up and down the line for hundreds of kilometers. To humans, who are forever talking, it almost seems that the storms are conversing in some secret code. The signals are split second — and spectacular.

DAY FOUR

Our orbit is shifting under the pull of Earth's gravity. The earth's bulge around the equator is tugging our orbit westward. Now we're beginning to see North America in daylight. Each pass into the night offers another spectacular sunset and sunrise of pure color. The sun's white disk splits into one rainbow beam after another. But our focus is still the delicate pastel earth below. Our daily sweep down the U.S. West Coast carries us over the deep green of California's forests. Some of the northern trees are thousands of years old. Nearby are the snowcapped Cascade volcanoes, including Crater Lake and the sleeping Mt. Shasta, which erupted less than a century ago.

Mt. Rainier, at the center of this radar image, last erupted about 150 years ago. Today the volcano is covered with glaciers and snowfields. In the last century, many large floods and mudflows have begun on its slopes. More than 100,000 people live on volcanic mudflows around this volcano. Space radar images may help to warn them of upcoming danger.

Waiting to Flood

Our radar target is the snow-covered Sierra Nevada range, where we will map the snowy peaks at Mammoth Lake, California. The radar map will not only tell us how much of the mountain range is snow-covered, but the amount of water locked up in the snowpack. That measurement will help warn of danger to California's central valley from spring flooding. It will also help predict how much water farmers will have for crop irrigation in the coming season. If we could put our radar into permanent orbit, we could eventually make these predictions for the entire planet, helping farmers and preserving lives and property.

Our earth is a water planet. While we usually think of the earth's waters as being open oceans, in space it's easy to see the influence water has on our biosphere. Wetlands, the places where water and land interact in marshes and along coast-lines, are also important to understanding the earth's climate. On our SRL mission we looked repeatedly at two wetland regions, the Amazon basin in Brazil and the Yucatán peninsula in Mexico.

The rain forests of the Amazon near Manaus, Brazil, flood every April during the rainy season, as the rivers spill out of their banks and into the rain forest. Similar rain-forest flooding occurs on the low-lying Yucatán peninsula in Central America. Both these swampy forests produce huge amounts of methane gas from wet, decaying vegetation. Methane is a powerful greenhouse gas. As it accumulates in the atmosphere, it traps heat, just like carbon dioxide. Knowing how much methane is released — and how much heat is trapped — is vital to our ability to predict climate changes on our planet.

The S-shaped bend in this radar image shows two sections of the Missouri River flood plain — Lisbon Bottoms and Jameson Island — where levees broke in the floods of 1993.

Breathing Trees

At the end of my shift, after North America has spun back around into sunlight, I get a glimpse of morning on the East Coast of the United States. As we soar northward up the coast, we scan the forests from North Carolina to Maine along the spine of the Appalachians. Our radar will be able to measure the leaf area and the amount of carbon in the trunks of these trees. This measurement of leaf area is important. With it, scientists can determine exactly how much carbon dioxide (from fires, pollution, etc.) these trees can convert to oxygen. On the ground, researchers, including students, are making spot measurements in these same forests. That way we can check to make sure the radar is accurate.

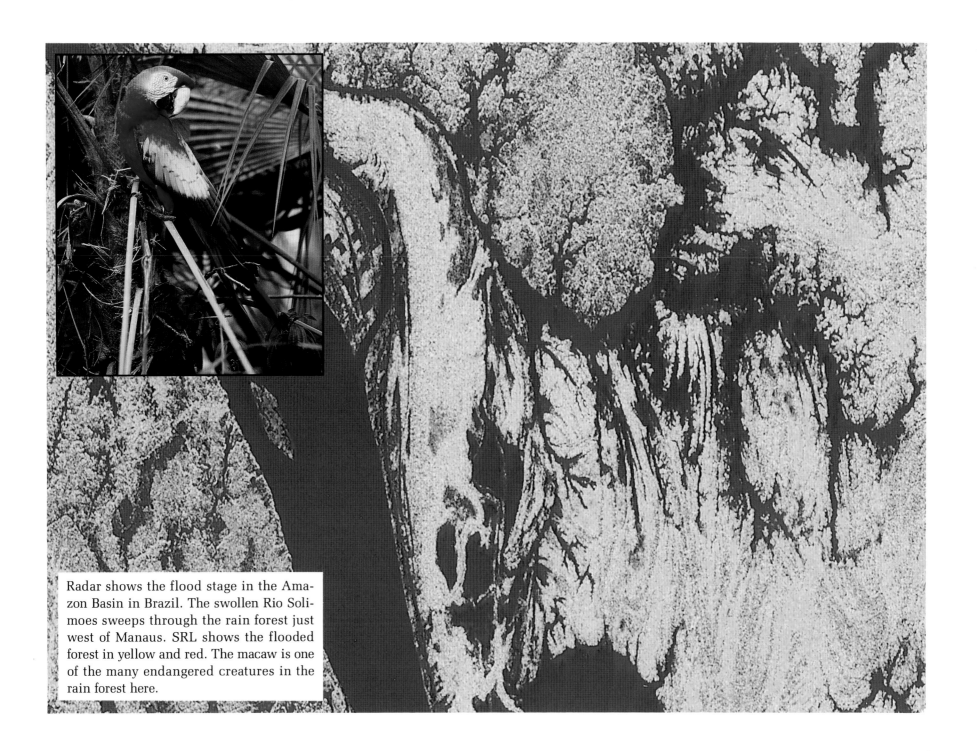

Radar shows the flood stage in the Amazon Basin in Brazil. The swollen Rio Solimoes sweeps through the rain forest just west of Manaus. SRL shows the flooded forest in yellow and red. The macaw is one of the many endangered creatures in the rain forest here.

Two radar images show Europe's varied landscape. One-quarter of this region of Austria (above) is covered by glaciers. It is one of the most important glacier research spots in the world. Below is a view of Flevoland in the Netherlands. Blue squares show cropland used for agriculture and forestry.

DAY FIVE

Spirits are high aboard *Endeavour*. We've completed four days of radar and pollution mapping, and all of our science instruments are humming with activity.

At night, our attention turns to the storms that loft carbon monoxide into the upper atmosphere. We darken the cockpit to better see the lightning. The view of flashing bolts lighting up the otherwise invisible thunderheads surpasses anything spun out of a movie special-effects shop.

Gazing down at the Mississippi Valley, I catch a meteor streaking below us into the atmosphere, burning a white-hot gash in the darkness, and leaving a faint glowing trail of ionized gas in its wake. The flash is too sudden to point out to anyone else on the crew. So it remains my own personal memory to carry with me from my first voyage in space.

Farms From Space

Our northernmost daylight passes shift to Europe now. For the bulk of the day my crewmates on the Blue Shift focus on a number of sites where scientists have made ground measurements to see if our space radar information is correct.

Today most of Europe is cloud-covered. But that doesn't stop our radar. It "sees" right through the clouds, painting a picture of the terrain below. Over the flat Dutch countryside, we spot the rich farms of Flevoland. Our radar images are able to distinguish between the fields of grain, vegetables, and flowers growing below.

At Oetztal in the Austrian Alps, we map the shifting positions of glaciers. We also look for the impact humans have had on these high alpine valleys. This delicate landscape has recently become a popular recreation area. The arrival of condominiums, skiers, and hikers has begun to threaten this fragile ecosystem. Our images of mountain vegetation will show us the areas hardest hit.

Aftermath of a Volcano

Before the flight, some of the most exciting work we'd done had been on volcanoes. Our training took us to the northwestern corner of the continental U.S., to Mt. Saint Helens. Twelve years before, a massive explosion had ripped the north side of the mountain apart. Already, hints of new green life were sprouting around the ash-coated base of the crater.

In orbit, nearly half a world away from Washington state now, we are probing the muddy ash deposits of another volcano — Mt. Pinatubo in the Philippines. When Pinatubo erupted in 1991, the explosion blew a huge dust cloud into the atmosphere that persisted into 1994. At the summit we can now make out the small green lake filling the still-steaming crater. The ash flows from the 1991 eruption are easy to see, their cement-gray tendrils standing out against the deep-green jungle and farmland.

The area around Pinatubo hadn't had time to recover the way Mt. Saint Helens had. Mudflows pouring down the sides of the mountain continue to smash villages and destroy farms. The situation around the mountain is still decidedly dangerous. Our radar images will help volcanologists better predict the activity around Pinatubo in the upcoming months.

Ash from the 1991 eruption of Mt. Pinatubo in the Philippines is represented in red in this radar image. The dark flows farther from the crater are rivers of muddy ash that are still destroying farms and villages along the mountain's flanks.

DAY SIX

Today's flight plan was crammed full of maneuvers, positioning *Endeavour* at the proper angle to "read" our radar sites. We have a mapping camera, the Linhof, fixed in the starboard overhead window, aimed at the same spot as the radar. It will help us record any weather conditions that may be affecting our radar imaging. The Linhof has an insatiable appetite for film, firing away with machine-gun repetition. Each night after going off duty we have to reload the Linhof magazines: Jay is the acknowledged ace at this chore. His skill leaves me more time to look out the window!

Clinging to a line of volcanoes, the bamboo forest habitat of the mountain gorilla is seen as a green band on the slopes at left center. The gorilla's habitat is just south of Lake Kivu, at top.

Rivers Beneath the Desert

Our big job today is taking a look at the Sahara. Our goal is to use the radar to probe beneath the tan and yellow sands of the Sahara and Arabian deserts. We're searching for bedrock that will provide clues to Earth's past climate. To our eyes and cameras, these vast stretches of sand seem featureless and impossible to see through. But the longest of our radar wavelengths ignores the dry sand and reflects off the hard rock beneath.

The map of ancient rivers we get from the radar images will tell us how long it has been since water flowed across the once grassy plains of northern Africa. Under Egypt's desert, scientists guided by space radar have already discovered remnants of ancient human habitation. One of the items I'd brought aboard the *Endeavour* was a 200,000-year-old stone ax discovered in the Sahara on the banks of one of these ancient "radar rivers."

Using information from these images, scientists may get clues about the current climate of Africa. This continent continues to lose more range and cropland to expanding deserts. The result is less food for Africa's growing population, keeping threatened countries at the brink of starvation.

South of the Sahara, rains turn Africa green again. SRL peers through the mists cloaking a line of volcanoes in Rwanda. We are mapping the shrinking bamboo-forest home of the mountain gorillas. Three hundred of these gentle creatures, half of their total number, survive on the rain-drenched slopes here. We hope to track human-caused changes in their habitat that threaten the last of these animals left on Earth.

Only a few hundred of these magnificent creatures have survived in the war-torn area in and around Rwanda.

DAY SEVEN

We've just turned things over to Sid, Linda, and Kevin on the Red Shift. It's been a tiring day — I hardly have the energy to describe the sights we've seen. What makes you tired in orbit when you don't weigh a thing? It's not my muscles that are tired, since they're used to microgravity by now. But my brain sure gets worn out after a long day of running a spaceship.

We *race* against the clock, because each radar-pointing pirouette of *Endeavour*, each data cassette change, each photo pass must be done *on time*. If we miss that planned start time, the chance to image some important piece of our planet is gone for this mission.

Because we do all our photography by daylight, we time our breaks for our sweeps over Earth's night side. We eat our lunch on the fly, in darkness over the Pacific, while the radar tracks storm waves below. We even time our trips to the bathroom so that we'll be ready for that important shot as the sun comes up.

Maybe I'm more tired today because of my exercise stint on the "stationary" bike this morning — it also orbits at eight kilometers a second! The exercise keeps our hearts and limb muscles in shape in microgravity. While the Red Shift slept, and Rich and Jay handled the science chores, I cycled halfway round the world.

Space Dreams

We saw much more of America today. While the Red Shift has been seeing our country almost daily, it's a new experience for us. Our target was the Mahantango watershed in Pennsylvania's Appalachian Mountains. The radar's job is to measure the soil moisture on the mountain ridges and valley farms. If the radar works as it should, we'll be able to advise farmers about the right soil conditions for planting. We'll also be able to predict the severity of floods from storm runoff in watershed streams.

Just half an orbit later we are immersed again in the greenish-white streamers of the aurora, between New Zealand and Australia. I feel ghostly shivers as we fly over and through the pulsating ribbons of light. Before bed, dinner of shrimp cocktail, spaghetti, potatoes au gratin, asparagus, and banana pudding. Then, snuggled into my bunk with a full stomach, sleep comes easily — there are no bad dreams in space.

DAY EIGHT

Endeavour's crew has finished a week in space. We've filled three fourths of our tape lockers with cassettes crammed full of radar data. Each one carries 35,000 times the information that can fit on a home computer diskette.

Skylights in Hawaii

A shuttle flight can never have too many volcano passes, and to add another to our tally we catch one on a night pass over the central Pacific. We can't see Kilauea's lava spilling into the Pacific in the darkness, but to compensate we get glittering views of the lights of Honolulu on Oahu and those on the smaller island of Kauai to the northwest.

Linda and I had vivid memories of visiting Kilauea on a research venture the previous year. The volcano has been erupting nearly continuously since 1983. On the island, we climbed over fresh lava flows below Kilauea's summit. At dusk, we stepped carefully over cracks in the new rock, glowing orange from lava running down to the ocean beneath us. We found holes in these lava tubes, called "skylights," where we could see white-hot lava streaming by at over 1,000 degrees C.

Centuries of such lava flows had created all of the Hawaiian Islands and this new eruption was building more land as we watched. Shielding our faces, we stabbed the bright yellow, taffylike lava with our hammers. We watched as it sputtered from orange to red to a dull black, turning to solid stone before our eyes.

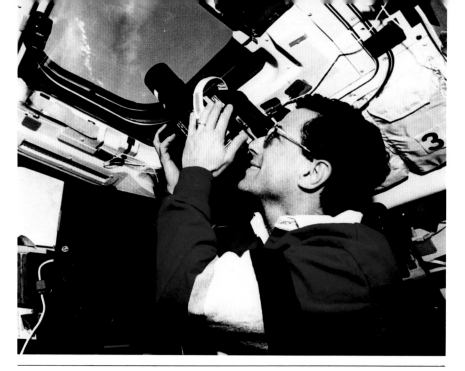

Jay Apt ran the Blue, or night shift, on *Endeavour*'s flight deck. Experienced in geography, and shuttle photography from his previous flights, Jay kept track of all our camera gear, and made sure it ran smoothly through the entire mission. Our success in bringing back 12,000 photos of the planet was due to his planning.

Ash and lava (seen in purple) from two centuries of eruptions can be seen in this radar image of the Mt. Kilauea volcano in Hawaii. Old lava flows are visible by radar even though the land may be covered with forest.

Rich Clifford was *Endeavour's* flight engineer and our crew's jack-of-all-trades. Nothing we encountered in orbit could suppress his broad grin and enthusiasm for the experience of space flight. Rich was the constant companion and steadfast friend of the only rookie on SRL-1 — me!

DAY NINE

The highlight of each day in orbit is a letter from home — about 12,000 miles away, give or take a few thousand. The realization that we have a fiery reentry to go through before we can actually get back down to Earth makes home seem very far away sometimes. When I have time to think about it, just before going to sleep each night, I have some feelings of homesickness in space. So mail from my wife Liz and my kids, Annie and Bryce, is always a treat.

Mail comes up by radio as a computer file. It appears on our screens along with other news each day as "the morning mail." Just before turning in each night we steal a few moments to send a short reply home. I also spend a few minutes in my bunk talking into a tape recorder to help me write this story.

By this point in the mission, the sleep periods of the Red and Blue shifts have moved so that we can spend about five hours in a row awake together, compared with only two or three earlier in the flight. More time together makes for more space recreation. Rich practices spinning me end-over-end in microgravity. I spend some spare time improvising a blow gun so I can shoot malted milk balls into the mouths of my fellow astronauts.

The extra time together also lets us do some crew sightseeing (daylight passes over America are our favorites). The fact that we've been successful in collecting all of our data has given everyone's spirits a huge boost. These last days in orbit are the best we've had thus far.

Our view shifted westward today to the central U.S., where we are measuring soil moisture in the alfalfa and wheat fields of southern Oklahoma. On the ground near the little town of Chickasha is a team of hydrologists (experts on Earth's water cycle). They are evaluating our information, comparing the radar measurements we radio back with their on-site data.

It rained in Chickasha early in the flight and in each of our daily passes we are able to see the wet soil drying out a little bit more under the spring sun. This is exactly the kind of measurement we need to help farmers getting ready to plant or harvest their crops. We are taking similar measurements in the Netherlands, France, Germany, and Australia.

Australia is of special interest. At Kerang, we not only measure soil moisture, but soil salinity, or saltiness. Our radar can tell salt- from freshwater because the dissolved salt affects how strongly the water reflects radar energy back to *Endeavour*.

Here at Kerang, salty groundwater is seeping into valuable pastureland, killing the grass and making it unfit for raising sheep or cattle. By mapping the extent of salt-caused damage, we hope to give ranchers some warning that their land is in danger. In response, they can plant more salt-resistant grasses and trees.

DAY TEN

By now, our science supersites are familiar to us from space. I can also recognize cities in the United States, even at night. On one pass up the East Coast of the United States, I spot the familiar lights of Washington and Baltimore laced together by delicate spiderwebs of interconnected highways. (After land-

ing, I would learn that my brother Ken in Virginia had seen us streak overhead just before sunrise while he waited for the 6:30 train to Alexandria. In the time it took him to get to his office, I'd gone all the way round the world!)

Endeavour is still running smoothly, but our science equipment is beginning to show the stress of nonstop work. One of our three high-speed data recorders has failed. We still have a spare, though, if needed. One of our two large Linhof mapping cameras has also jammed. Luckily, we are almost out of film.

Fires Below, Pollution Above

The MAPS pollution sensor continues to run smoothly around the clock, taking carbon monoxide measurements once every second as we circle the globe. During our night passes we are continuing to report fires for MAPS, mainly in South America and Africa.

At one point early in the mission, the MAPS scientists were

Viewed at night from space, the east coast cities of the U.S. show up as an interconnected web of light. This radar image reveals details of New York City. The green-colored rectangle on Manhattan Island is Central Park.

puzzled by the high levels of carbon monoxide in a band stretching across the Atlantic from Cape Horn in South America to the Cape of Good Hope at the southern tip of Africa. This area is almost completely open ocean — no fires or industry in sight. After searching around for clues, we finally solved the mystery from orbit. We sighted a cluster of bright fires near Tierra del Fuego, Argentina. The MAPS team checked with a scientist in the area. He identified the fires as burning flares of natural gas from an offshore oil field. This was most likely the source of all the carbon monoxide rising into the upper atmosphere.

DAY ELEVEN

Our mission to planet Earth is almost over. We shut down one of our three radars last night. Today we'll close down the rest of the Space Radar Lab and get ready to come home. While the Red Shift (including our shuttle pilots, Sid and Kevin) sleeps, Rich, Jay, and I start packing up the cabin for entry into the atmosphere.

All of the camera gear and computers have to be packed away in *Endeavour's* storage lockers. Rich stows away the last of the radar data tapes downstairs. We've gone through 166 tapes, all full of images of the home planet. Jay squeezes a few last rolls of film into our lower bunk with the rest of the 12,000 photos we'd taken during the course of our ten days in space.

From the air lock, we bring out the six orange space suits that we'll wear for reentry. They'll protect us if a cabin leak dumps our air overboard during the 45-minute ride back to Florida.

One Last Pass

About six hours prior to landing, I turn off the radar electronics and the power and cooling sources that kept them humming for ten days. The Space Radar Lab is now hibernating, waiting for its next flight in the fall.

With our science work complete, we have a few free hours just to relax and look out the window. With no film to shoot and no radars to tend, Rich and I float with our backs to the floor. One last trip around the earth, this time recorded imperfectly, but vividly, in my own memory.

Endeavour's voyage — and its crew's — has gone very well. We began in Asia, mapping the cover of snow and ice on the plains and lakes of Siberia. We scanned forests, too, just as they were awakening from their long winter's sleep, their needles standing dark against the melting snow. Farther east, we plotted the sea ice in the Sea of Okhotsk, a dazzling white crust on the deep blue of the ocean, stray shards of ice drifting toward Kamchatka peninsula and the islands of Japan.

I will never forget the great deserts of central Asia, either. Here we penetrated the dust storms with our radar, searching for ancient villages and climates buried beneath the tan and yellow sands. The landscape of Earth was varied and dramatic, but it was also fragile. In India and Burma, we watched smoke plumes from farm clearings gather to a great pall that covered an entire mountain range.

On the island of Borneo off southeast Asia, we peered between towering thunderstorms. Here there was evidence of

Sometimes memories are better captured with the eye than a camera. I get one last dazzling view of the home planet from *Endeavour*'s flight deck.

deforestation as a growing population is pushing inland from the crowded coast. As we soared overhead, the clouds obscured our view of the jungle. But the radar would clearly record the scene, tree by tree.

The most dramatic scene in the Pacific islands, though, was Mt. Pinatubo in the Philippines. While the radar scanned its ash deposits and lava flows our crew absorbed the sprawl of destruction from above where, three short years before, nearly eight cubic kilometers of ash and lava had blasted from the now quiet mountain. We marveled at the blanket of ash coating the countryside, and the mud-choked river channels snaking in all directions from the mountain to the sea. Nestled within the crater like a set jewel, a turquoise lake covered the volcanic vent.

We visited glaciers in the southern Andes and rain forests in the Amazon basin. The ultimate globetrotters, we would circle the world 183 times. It had been the adventure of a lifetime, but one I hoped to repeat.

Looking for a Landing

In just a short hour, we go from pure relaxation to frenzy, as we swing into our reentry tasks. Sid, the commander; Kevin, the pilot; and Rich, our flight engineer, focus on preparing the orbiter's systems and computers for entry. I handle switches and circuit breakers in the rear of the cockpit, and close the payload bay doors over SRL, sealing the cargo from the heat of entry. Downstairs, Jay helps our payload commander, Linda, get us suited up. Late in our workday now, we are ready to fire the two maneuvering engines to slow us down enough to break orbit.

Unfortunately, the weather isn't cooperating in Florida. We wait through two orbits for a break in the clouds. Finally Mission Control in Houston cancels our Tuesday landing and tells us to try again tomorrow. Rich, Jay, and I scramble out of our suits and into bed for a short night's sleep.

Through the Fire

Next day, Florida's weather again refuses to cooperate. So we retarget our landing to California, where blue skies await us. We can barely feel the engines fire at *Endeavour*'s tail, but twenty minutes after that gentle nudge we've slowed enough to arc back into the atmosphere over the central Pacific. From my seat behind Kevin on the flight deck, I'm treated to one last space show: *Endeavour*'s front windows are bathed in an orange-pink glow. At our speed of 25 times the speed of sound, friction strips apart the superheated air molecules outside *Endeavour*. Our passage creates a fiery trail behind our overhead windows. From my seat, this intense plume looks like the purple and yellow heart of a blowtorch flame.

Soon we experience the unfamiliar sensation of weight. As *Endeavour* turns to line up with the Edwards Air Force Base runways, we feel the pull of one and a half times the force of gravity. This small extra tug, though, makes me feel as if I weigh 400 pounds! Just holding up my video camera takes all my strength. As my muscles fight to readapt to gravity, Sid gently lowers *Endeavour*'s tires to the California runway. *Endeavour* is home.

Endeavour glides onto the runway at Edwards Air Force Base in California, returning with thousands of images of Earth. Technicians quickly readied *Endeavour* for the SRL-2 mission just six months later.

Mt. Klyuchevskaya in full eruption, October 1994. SRL-2 had the good luck to launch on the very day the tallest volcano in Asia exploded into life.

A synopsis of mission facts for *STS-68*:

LAUNCH DATE/SITE:	September 30, 1994/ Kennedy Space Center PAD 39A
LAUNCH TIME:	7:16 A.M. EDT
ORBITER:	*Endeavour*
ORBIT/INCLINATION:	120 nautical miles/57 degrees
MISSION DURATION:	11 days, 5 hours, 46 minutes, 9 seconds
LANDING TIME/DATE:	1:02 P.M. EDT October 11, 1994
LANDING SITE:	Edwards Air Force Base, California
***STS-68* CREW:**	Michael Baker, Commander
	Terrence Wilcutt, Pilot
	Thomas D. Jones, Payload Commander
	Steven Smith, Mission Specialist 1
	Daniel Bursch, Mission Specialist 2
	Jeff Wisoff, Mission Specialist 3
	Red Shift: Baker, Wilcutt, Wisoff
	Blue Shift: Bursch, Jones, Smith
Cargo Bay Payloads:	Space Radar Laboratory 2 (SRL-2)

Space Radar Lab 2

Our science team was eager to follow up the success of SRL-1 with a look at Earth in a completely different season. So *Endeavour*'s next flight, just four months later, would carry the Space Radar Lab into orbit again. We wanted to look again at all our science sites, watching for changes in the environment. Would pollution patterns be different? Were ocean currents shifting directions? How much more rain forest had we lost? *Endeavour* and its crew were ready again on August 18, 1994, but just a half-second before booster ignition and lift-off, our computers detected an overheating main engine. Faster than any human could react, they shut down all three engines, stopped the countdown, and prevented us from leaving Earth with a potentially dangerous problem.

The next attempt was six weeks later, on September 30, 1994. This time the countdown was perfect, and Space Radar Lab 2 soared into orbit for 11 days of intense scrutiny of planet Earth. We saw obvious changes in snow cover and vegetation patterns from April — spring had turned to summer and fall in the northern hemisphere. We could easily see how fires set by humans had intensified in South America and the tropics of Asia, creating a pall of smoke and haze that obscured our view of the surface in those areas. (Our radar abilities were unaffected.) The highlight of our second mission was witnessing the violent eruption of the Klyuchevskaya volcano in far northeast Asia. *Endeavour* was in perfect position for our camera and radar images to track the entire course of the eruption for geologists back on Earth. This remote volcano's week-long eruption was the most spectacular example of natural change we captured on either flight, a perfect illustration of the value of observing Earth from space. By mission's end, we'd gathered even more radar images and shot more film than on our first successful flight.

These two missions proved so productive, and showed such potential for Earth monitoring, that NASA and its partners in Germany and Italy are planning a third Space Radar Lab flight. The goal of SRL-3, which may fly in 1998, will be to create a radar map of almost all Earth's land surface. The new map will include not only the positions of geographic features like mountains and rivers, but also their elevation. Today, no such map exists. SRL-3 will provide the fine level of detail needed to map the changes in the environment we saw on the first two Space Radar Lab flights, and will give our planet a "checkup" three years after we captured the views you see here.

The *STS-68* astronauts leave their crew quarters at Kennedy Space Center for SRL-2, September 30, 1994. Left to right: Bursch, Wisoff, Smith, Wilcutt, Jones, and Baker.

The Mission to Planet Earth Continues

The SRL missions will help scientists prepare for the next phase of the Mission to Planet Earth. Phase II will begin in 1998 with the launch of the first Earth Observing System (EOS) Satellite. A total of 17 satellites will eventually be put into space to keep track of changes on the planet. With the information gained from them and other ground systems, a 15-year-long environmental database will be created.

Once the system is in place, environmental scientists throughout the world will have access to this data, as will international governments. With this information, people throughout the world will be able to make informed decisions about dangers to the environment.

During the past twenty years, satellites have recorded the changing ozone layer over Earth. The key on the right shows the colors used to illustrate the density or thickness of ozone. The ozone layer is thinnest where it appears as purple or black.

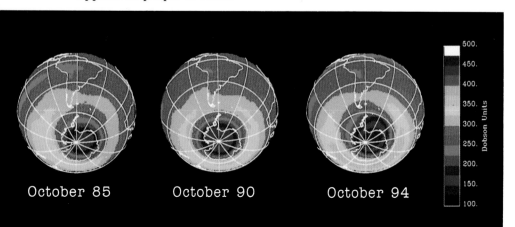

October 85   October 90   October 94

On this page and those following are descriptions of some of the environmental issues that the Space Radar Lab and the Mission to Planet Earth will continue to explore.

THE AIR WE BREATHE (ATMOSPHERE)

When *Endeavour* returned to Earth, it dropped through the 100-mile-thick layer of gases that surround the planet. Billions of years ago, Earth's atmosphere was made up of an odd assortment of noxious gases including ammonia and methane — enough to scorch the lungs of human or beast. But the atmosphere, like Earth and the living things on it, evolved into a gentler form.

Today the delicate balance of temperatures and gases in the layers of atmosphere makes our lives possible. Humans, animals, and plants rely on this envelope to allow us to breathe and grow — that is, as long as the balance of gases is preserved. Large amounts of pollutants in the atmosphere can make the air around us less healthy, sometimes even deadly.

Automobile exhaust and burning of cropland put large amounts of carbon dioxide (CO_2) and carbon monoxide (CO) into the air. Carbon dioxide alone can warm our atmosphere, but the carbon monoxide can worsen the problem. Carbon monoxide molecules use up hydroxyls, which neutralize other gases that might cause the earth to overheat. Added carbon monoxide means there may not be enough hydroxyl molecules to cleanse the air.

The MAPS instrument carried aboard *Endeavour* measured carbon monoxide levels at thousands of sites around the planet. Some were taken over urban areas like Toronto and Moscow, others over areas where large-scale agricultural fires were burning. To make a comparison, carbon monoxide readings were also taken in places where the air is quite clean, such as New Zealand.

Using these measurements, scientists can figure out how much carbon monoxide and other harmful gases are released by different sources of pollution. As Mission to Planet Earth continues, other instruments on satellites are already testing the air. These satellites will also help predict climate changes caused by pollution. Serious air pollution problems throughout the world can be identified and eventually eliminated.

THE WATER WE DRINK (HYDROLOGY)

On the edge of an African savannah, small patches of crops wither and die, worsening famine across the continent. At the very same moment, heavy rainfall in California turns to floods, collapsing houses and bridges and causing deadly mud slides.

These two events are part of one large story, the story of water on our planet. Water undergoes an endless cycle that ties our planet together. Moisture from the soil evaporates and forms clouds in the atmosphere. Clouds form raindrops that descend to Earth and seep into the soil, renewing the cycle.

Several supersites on *Endeavour*'s tour were devoted to watersheds, areas where water — whether in soil, rain, or snowfall — eventually drains into a river, like the Amazon. The watershed controls the delivery of water to forests, farms,

A fleet of clouds brings rare rainfall to the Tifernine Dunes of the Sahara desert.

and cities. In Oklahoma, measurements were taken to find out how fast farmland dries out after a rainstorm. In the Sierra Nevada and at Mt. Everest, winter snow was measured to predict spring runoff.

Taking snow measurements from space is a huge improvement over older methods. Space radar can give an instant measure of the amount of snow and the water contained in the snow. And it can relate those measurements at a million points simultaneously!

The extent of snowpack is also important in determining whether the overall climate of the planet is changing. Measurements of glacier movements repeated over several seasons can give an idea if the planet is heating up or cooling off.

In the future, Mission to Planet Earth satellites will use longer microwave wavelengths to measure rainfall from space. Hydrologists hope to set up a comprehensive model of how the earth's entire water system works.

Dark tones in the center of this radar image show ice fields in the Andes covered with thick wet snow. Outlet glaciers, in yellow and purple, are seen calving into the dark water of lakes and fiords.

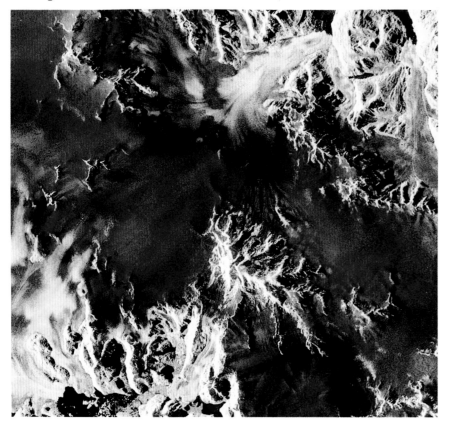

THE OCEANS AROUND US (OCEANOGRAPHY)

If you could pump out the 700 million cubic miles of water that fill the world's oceans, you'd see a magnificent landscape. Underneath the watery depths are higher mountains, deeper canyons, and wider valleys than anything on the earth's dry surfaces.

One of the targets for the Space Radar Lab was the Southern Ocean. Of all the waters on earth, the Southern Ocean is the least known, most fascinating — and the most dangerous. Off the coast of southern Africa waves routinely join together to create giant rogue waves that can crest at 40 feet or more. Such powerful waves, running one on top of another, can swamp a supertanker. During the flights of *Endeavour*, SRL provided ten days of complete information about the sea surface, waves, and storms in this ocean surrounding Antarctica.

Ocean water is never still, and its movements carry energy in the form of heat to the ends of the earth. Currents such as the Gulf Stream are so powerful they can change the climate of an area. In southwestern Britain, farther north than Quebec, you can find thriving palm trees and gentle winters. The oceans not only carry weather, they create it. Where warmer or colder water currents meet the air above, they create clouds or fog. Upwellings flush cold water up to the ocean's surface and create a fertile environment for schools of fish. The ocean, in a very real sense, controls the pattern of climate and life across the entire planet.

Yet for all of their grandeur, the oceans of this planet are fragile. Changes in salt, mineral, and chemical content can

Typhoon Odessa as seen from STS-51. Shuttle views of tropical cyclones can show the three-dimensional structure of these storms much better than weather satellites.

damage the balance of life in ocean water. Plastics, petroleum products, and other pollution in the water can damage the immune systems of animals or wipe out fish populations entirely. Along the southern California coast, the temperature of the ocean water has risen about two to three degrees in recent years. As a result much of the zooplankton has died. The multitudes of fish that feed on these tiny animals, and the seabirds that feed on the fish, have disappeared.

For the past decade NASA has used satellite and shuttle instruments to chart the world's oceans. Observations from satellites and the space shuttle now keep track of temperatures all over the ocean. They can also chart currents and eddies. By comparing information taken in the future with these readings, researchers can tell if any major changes have taken place, and even what is causing these changes. The oceans may provide the earliest clues about whether humans are changing the earth's climate.

Sea ice swirls in the Labrador Current, off the coast of Newfoundland, Canada.

THE CHANGING EARTH (GEOLOGY)

One of the most remarkable traits of the Space Radar Lab is its ability to make exact three-dimensional maps of Earth. During the SRL flights, several sites were identified for interferometry, or space mapping. Exact maps are useful for everyone from scientists to city planners. But the accuracy of this type of radar can potentially save lives.

Earthquakes and volcanoes show that the earth is always changing, sometimes in a split second, and sometimes drastically. These severe changes in earth's landscape, especially earthquakes, are very difficult to predict. In this century alone, 1,500,000 people have died in earthquakes. They continue to plague large populations in threatened cities all over the world.

The Space Radar Lab's ability to map the earth's surface may eventually provide a warning system for natural disasters such as earthquakes and volcanoes. Since the radar can pick up very tiny changes in the land — even a centimeter's difference — it can show slippage that might result in quakes, or bulging that may warn of a volcanic eruption.

SRL's geology mission did more than make maps. Passes over the Sahara showed how this desert now covers riverbeds where water once flowed. The earth's deserts are created by weather patterns, influenced by the nearby terrain. Today over 30 percent of the earth's land is desert. And that area is growing.

Some of this expansion of desert may be caused by the earth gradually growing warmer. But the expansion of deserts is also due to overgrazing of animals or other human activities

Ten miles above Earth, the jet stream carries Klyuchevskaya's ash and steam plume out over the Pacific.

that damage vegetation. This effect is called "desertification." Desertification is dangerous because the bigger a desert gets the more farm and range land is lost.

The Sahara is already bigger than the entire continental United States. (Imagine traveling across the U.S. if it were completely desert!) As the Sahara spreads at its edges, the loss of useful crop and ranching areas can be huge. Africa, a continent plagued by drought and an exploding population, can scarcely afford to lose an acre of cropland.

Irrigation, though it tries to solve the problem of dryness, sometimes actually makes things worse. A body of water that separates two dry areas may actually help to keep each of those areas from becoming a real desert. The presence of a river, for instance, helps form clouds that produce rainfall. When the river is diverted for irrigation, rain clouds may diminish or disappear.

Space Radar Lab's investigations of how the earth has evolved can tell us more about which Earth changes are natural and which are caused by human activities. In the future the Mission to Planet Earth will focus on more of these climate records in Earth's landscape, and give us more information about our planet's past — and its future.

THE LIVING PLANET (ECOLOGY)

The biological richness of our planet is almost beyond the grasp of a human mind. We estimate that more than 10 million species of plants and animals live on our Earth. That includes over 10,000 tree species, 5 million insect species, and 5,000

other animal species. To realize how extraordinary this is, consider that not a single life-form has yet been identified on any other planet in our solar system. The earth is a biological gold mine in what seems a lifeless corner of the universe.

A lot of this treasure is jammed into some comparatively small parts of the planet. The wetlands of the earth are one example. Wetlands, in addition to acting as water purification plants, are also nurseries to many kinds of marine, amphibian, and bird life. Unfortunately, many of the wetlands of the world have disappeared in this century. Swamps, bogs, and marshes have been converted to farmland or drained and used as building sites. Many of these rich, irreplaceable breeding grounds have been lost. *Endeavour*'s radar, sensitive to standing water and swampy terrain, tested a technique for mapping our remaining wetland areas. A future radar observatory will, we hope, monitor these regions and point out those that face the most severe threats.

This rare albino alligator is native to the wetlands of the lower Mississippi.

Like wetlands, rain forests are home to a rich variety of plants and creatures. Five million species of plants and animals, about half of all living things, live in rain forests, areas with dense tree growth and heavy rainfall. A quarter of our prescription medicines come from products that grow in the rain forest. These areas are some of the richest biological resources on Earth. Yet in the Amazon, a football-field-sized plot of trees is cut and burned every minute. Native farmers need the land to grow crops or pasture cattle; others want to use the space for development.

As the trees are cut, animals and plants lose their habitats. Some native peoples, who use the forest for food and cash crops, are left without a way to live. As the vegetation is burned or decomposes, carbon dioxide is released into the

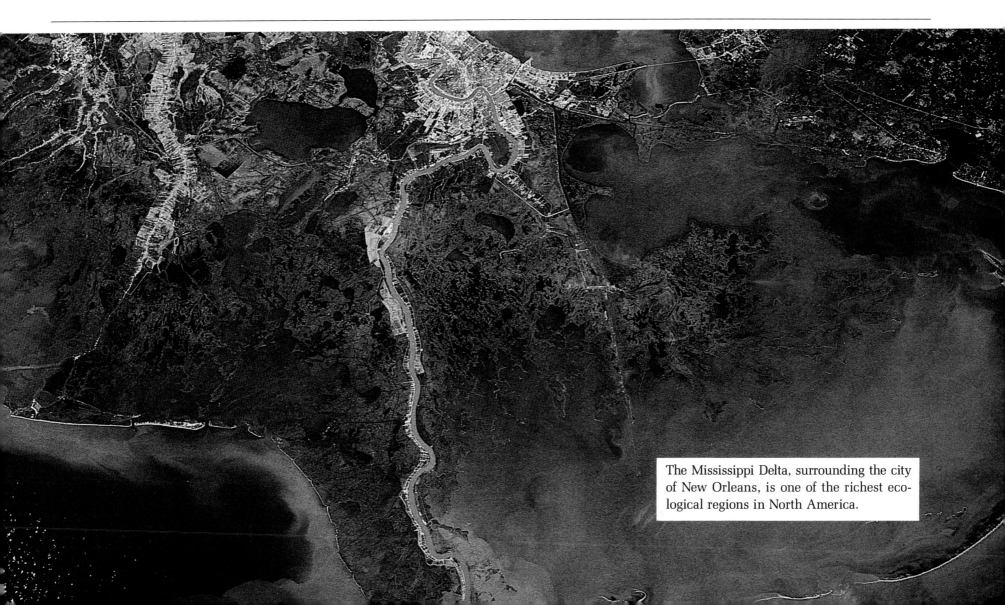

The Mississippi Delta, surrounding the city of New Orleans, is one of the richest ecological regions in North America.

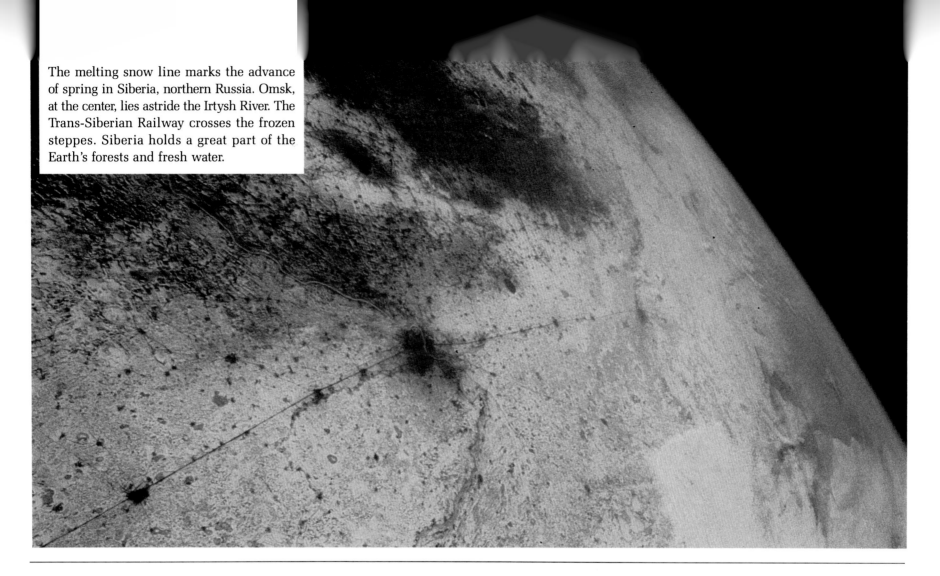

The melting snow line marks the advance of spring in Siberia, northern Russia. Omsk, at the center, lies astride the Irtysh River. The Trans-Siberian Railway crosses the frozen steppes. Siberia holds a great part of the Earth's forests and fresh water.

atmosphere along with other greenhouse gases. Rain forests, which provide much of the oxygen animals and humans need to live, are increasingly in peril.

But they are not the only great natural reserves on the planet. Siberian forests in northern Russia are so large they could contain all the rain forests on earth. For many years they have been nearly untouched. But because of their value as timber as well as the gold ore and oil beneath the forests, they are now in jeopardy. The forests of Siberia surround the deepest lake in the world, Lake Baikal, which contains nearly 20 percent of the world's freshwater.

By mapping and monitoring these areas, the Mission to Planet Earth will help to preserve them for our future and the future of Earth's children to come.

Last Words

A few years ago I opened my mailbox and found a picture postcard inside. On the front of the card was the word *Kansas* and a picture of a tornado. I turned it over and saw that it was from my childhood friend, Tom Jones. After a few sentences discussing his recent travels, he paused in the middle to tell me he was going into space.

Close behind came the news that I was actually going to see Tom blasted into space. I'd shortly be able to see a shuttle launch with someone I knew onboard. This surely wasn't Kansas anymore.

Some months later I arrived at the appointed time in a parking lot in Cocoa Beach, Florida. I handed over my blue night-viewing pass to the NASA official. She checked my name, looked me over, and finally allowed me to board the large blue bus with NASA painted on the side. The vehicle would ferry family and friends of the astronauts to see *Endeavour* before its launch the next morning. There were a lot of kids on the bus and a fair amount of noise and laughter as we drove down the back roads to launchpad 39A. The sun was just setting over the wetlands that sprawl behind the Space Center. We drove for about a half hour through green thickets dotted with tiny ponds and the odd piece of space hardware.

I was thrilled at the chance to get a night-viewing of *Endeavour* before the next day's launch. After several failed attempts to actually see a liftoff, this would be my first actual

launch. I'd waited a long time and somehow I knew it was now going to happen.

As we got closer to the launchpad I could see the crossed blue-white xenon lights outlining *Endeavour*, its rocket boosters, and rust-colored fuel tank. It was ready to go. So, undoubtedly, were Tom and the crew. But, I wondered, were the rest of us?

We turned into a small parking lot and the NASA official pulled out her microphone. "There's been a lot of rain here lately," she said. "I know you all want to get the best view of the orbiter for your cameras. But, please, stay on the cement and out of the fields and ditches. The extra rain means there are extra snakes and extra alligators."

I'd heard that they often had to chase alligators off the runway with a big broom when the shuttle came in for landing. And I'd seen those green eyes and cratered heads peeking up from the ditches along the highway. No arguments from me. I would stay on the cement. Others, however, were not convinced.

"There are people out in the ditches already," a family member called out as we started to get off the bus.

"Those are journalists," said the official. "They're expendable." She meant, I think, to say that though it was okay to lose a journalist or two, it wasn't okay to lose any of us. Since I had been a journalist for a while, I kept my head down. I'm all for wildlife preservation, but I didn't want to become part of the food chain, especially before the launch.

The orbiter was scrubbed-white and shining out on the pad. The launch tower was lit up by what looked like giant fairy lights. In the crossed xenon beams above the orbiter, white birds flew in an arc. They must have mistaken the beams for moonlight.

In a moment, a few of the astronauts walked out on the grass and people began to wave and applaud. Earlier in the day, during a tour, we had seen one of the astronauts pull up in a sports car. It was an utterly cool car, and he looked as if he had jumped out of the movie *The Right Stuff*.

Tonight, though, these astronauts looked altogether humanoid. They were all under quarantine and had to stand six feet away from us — the average distance of a sneeze. They looked a bit tired, maybe, but happy. Especially Tom.

I wonder if there is anyone on Earth who has ever been happier to get into space than Tom was. And no wonder. Like a shortwave radio ham, he had been listening to voices from space since he was a child. Perhaps they had been calling to him. In show-and-tell, when the rest of us brought in seashell collections, Tom brought in a scale model of the lunar lander. He was meant for space. Now, though, looking at that giant orbiter and knowing the explosive power it took to get it into space, it was hard not to worry a little. I kept thinking: How can they put a 12-year-old into *that*?

I was not alone in my worries. Tom's mother stood next to me, grimacing as Tom pointed out the crew area of the orbiter. "I'll be up there in just six hours."

Although she was trying hard, I could see that she was avoiding looking at *Endeavour*. It was a startling piece of machinery, but not something she wanted her son to crawl into. "I can't even watch planes from the backyard," she said. "I never fly."

I was plenty happy to see Tom's mother. She was someone

I could talk to. More importantly, she was wielding a can of insect repellent and I was being mercilessly attacked by squadrons of killer mosquitoes. Just across the field stood the pond named Mosquito Lagoon — not for nothing, I thought.

Soon it was time for the astronauts to go back to their quarters. They lingered a bit, not wanting to leave. We stood staring and waving as they finally said their good-byes. On the way back, there wasn't a lot of talking on the bus, just some sounds of sniffles as people stared out the window. Kids fell asleep on their mothers' shoulders. Some of their mothers had red eyes and were clutching tissues. As the bus drove back to Cocoa Beach in the dark, I had some time to think.

Tom's voyage on *Endeavour* would be part of NASA's Mission to Planet Earth. Like other astronauts he would travel into the wilds of space. But he wouldn't be looking for far-off galaxies, quasars, and black holes. Instead he would be looking at us, Earth, the home planet, the blue light in the void. He would be using a new kind of radar to pry under the sands of the Sahara, and to look inside volcanoes. He would be testing the air and photographing rain forests and oceans. With the information the *Endeavour* crew gathered, scientists could start to make sense of some of the environmental problems of our planet.

The mission was full of hope, yet some part of me was incredibly sad. Sometimes the problems of this planet seemed so big and overwhelming, as if nothing I, or anyone else, could do could help set it right again. Yet, there is still so much life on Earth, so much to be proud of, so much to protect. Just looking at this tiny corner of Florida, it was easy to see: the sweet-faced manatees and bald eagles, the orchids and coral reefs — all the plants and animals at risk of disappearing forever. Yet each one of them was magical, each one was worth all that we could do to keep it safe.

At five o'clock the next morning, I boarded another bus — this time to Banana Creek. As the clock counted down, we sat on wooden benches feeding sleepily on warm sugar donuts and black coffee. The silky waters of the creek lay in front of us and beyond stood the white shuttle pointing toward the sky. In the fresh water, striped bass leaped in the cool air as the sun lifted slowly above the horizon.

As we counted down the minutes to launch, I started thinking that the Mission to Planet Earth was maybe the most important space mission of all. It seemed somehow right that the shuttle was being launched from here, a space pad nestled in the middle of a wildlife preserve. Liquid hydrogen and blue herons, astronauts and alligators — we were all in this together.

June English
New York, NY

KANSAS

Countdown

At T minus 5 minutes, they pronounced all systems go.
Without Earth, there would be no checklists, no computers, no systems.
At T minus 2 minutes, wisps of hydrogen swirled from the orbiter.
Without Earth, there would be no rockets, no engines, no orbiter.

At T minus 0, the engines ignited, the solid rockets fired. The sound of
exploding fuel blossomed in the air.
Without Earth, there would be no ignition, no launch, no mission.
Like a comet, *Endeavour* flared into the sky.
Without Earth, there would be no us.

J.A.E.

INDEX

Note: Page numbers in *italics* indicate an illustration or photograph.

Photo Credits:

1: NASA; 3: NASA; 6: NASA STS 059-304-028; 8: NASA AS 11-44-6549; 9: NASA; 10: Courtesy Dornier Labs; 11: NASA STS 059-215-022; 13: NASA STS 059 (S) 034; 14 (left): NASA STS 059-19-004; 14 (right): NASA STS 059-13-030; 15: NASA STS 059-19-020; 16: NASA STS 059-71-098; 17 (left): NASA STS 068-08-029; 17 (right): NASA STS 059-82-010;/18: NASA; 19 (left): NASA STS 39-332-023; 19 (right): NASA P-44703; 20: NASA P-44733; 21: NASA; 21 (inset): Gerry Ellis; 22 (top): NASA P-44756; 22 (bottom): NASA P-43930; 23: NASA P-43915; 24: NASA P-44508; 25: Gerry Ellis; 26 (top): NASA STS 059-09-012; 26 (bottom): NASA STS 059-46-025; 27: NASA P-43918; 28: NASA P-45621; 30: STS 059-30-002; 31: NASA STS 059 (S) 107; 32: NASA STS 068-150-045; 33: NASA KSC-94 PC-1010; 34: NASA; 35: NASA STS 068-228-081; 36: NASA P-45740; 37: NASA 511-35-075; 38: NASA STS 39-80-063; 39: NASA STS 068-218-007; 40: Ping Amranand; 41: NASA 51C-143-0027; 42: NASA STS 059-215-033; 43: NASA KSC-94PC-291; 44: Tom Jones; 46: Courtesy The Kansas Postcard Co.; 47: NASA STS 068 (S) 027.

Prints of some of the Earth photographs in this book can be obtained from: Eros Data Center, User Services Section, Sioux Falls, South Dakota 57198. Use the NASA numbers above to inquire about specific photographs. NASA "P" numbered radar images can be viewed on the Internet at **http://southport.jpl.nasa.gov.** Examples of the best shuttle Earth photographs can be seen at **http://images.jsc.nasa.gov.**